King Akbar and The Shepherd

How Devotion Determines a Satsangi's Life

Adapted from a story told by Sant Ram Singh Ji, August 1, 2015

"No one has got liberated without devotion." Kabir Sahib

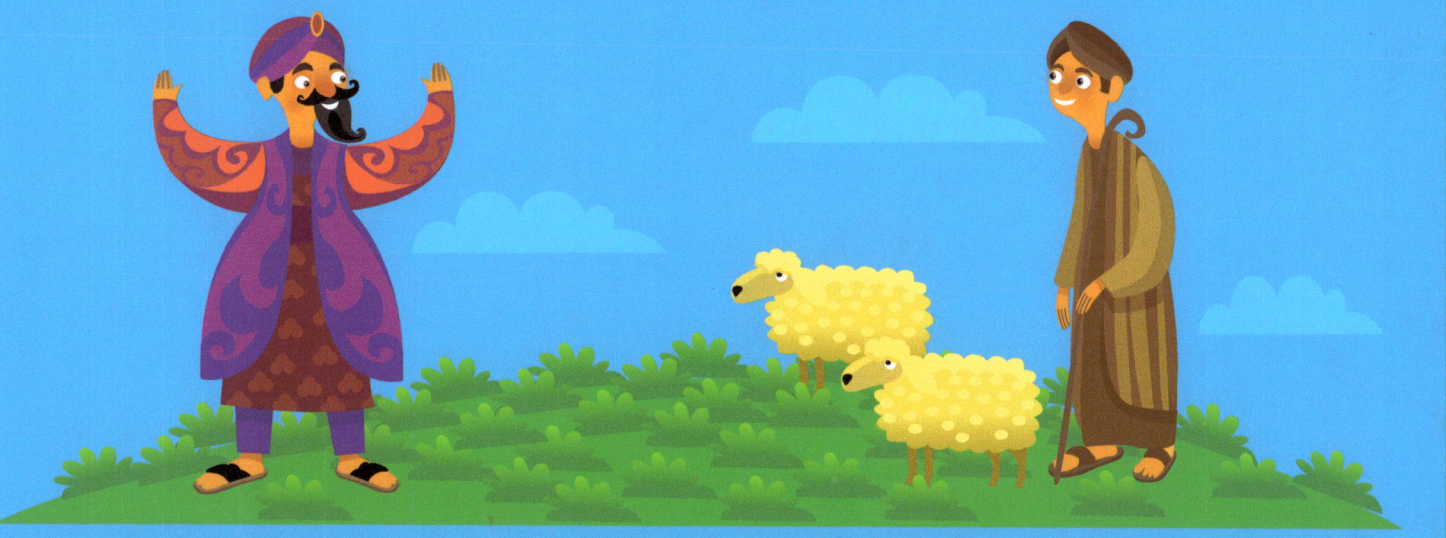

King Akbar and The Shepherd
How Devotion Determines a Satsangi's Life

King Akbar and The Shepherd
was originally told by
Sant Ram Singh Ji on August 1, 2015 at
Channasandra Ashram in India.

Special thanks to those who critiqued and reviewed the story:
Geoff Halstead,
Richard and Sharon Malarich.
Their suggestions have made the story
more accessible for children.

Translated by Ashok Shinkar
Transcribed by Ali Czernin, Geoff Halstead, & Harvey

Carlos Brito adds his beautiful, colorful, and fun illustrations,
which make the story more vibrant while bringing joy to our hearts and beauty to our souls.
Thank you, dear brother.

ISBN: 978-1-942937-07-4

Published by
Go Jolly Books
www.gojollybooks.com
74 Gem Ln., Sandpoint, ID 83864
FIRST EDITION, GO JOLLY BOOKS, First Printing 2016
10 9 8 7 6 5 4 3 2 1 Printed in the U.S.A.

King Akbar and The Shepherd

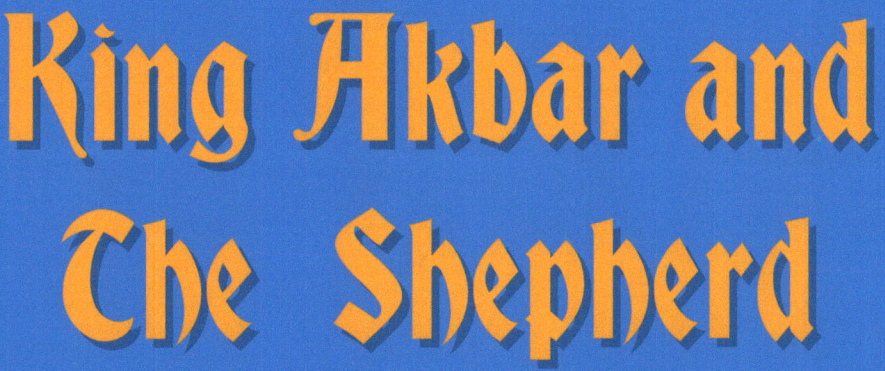

How Devotion Determines a Satsangi's Life

GO JOLLY BOOKS

INTRODUCTION

In January, 2014, at Channasandra Ashram in India, I asked Sant Ram Singh Ji if I could take stories He told in Satsang and publish them as books.

Although I don't recall His exact words, He said yes. Then He told me to make sure the books were for children. To me that meant I could substitute "Hindi words translated into English words" with "child-friendly English words" to make the story easier for children to understand. With His Limitless Grace, reviewers of the first two books have told us we have succeeded.

King Akbar and The Shepherd is the second story of Sant Ram Singh Ji that has been turned into a book. The first book was **The King and His Three Daughters.**

I hope you enjoy **King Akbar and The Shepherd:** How Devotion Determines a Satsangi's Life. It's been a joy watching Carlos Brito bring to life his colorful, unique illustrations, which add exceptional beauty to Sant Ram Singh Ji's story.

Radhaswami,
Harvey

King Akbar and The Shepherd

How Devotion Determines a Satsangi's Life

This book is dedicated to Sant Ram Singh Ji,
Whose Limitless Grace and Unconditional Love
shower upon us as only a
True Friend and Living Master can do.

Once upon a time, a King named Akbar went hunting in a jungle. After traveling about ten kilometers, he felt hungry. Poor people are accustomed to hunger but kings and other royalty who eat regularly cannot bear pangs of hunger.

King Akbar saw a shepherd and asked him if he had something to eat or drink. Shepherds usually bring food while caring for their sheep, and he agreed to share his food with Akbar.

They both sat down under a tree. The shepherd found a big leaf, cleaned it, then placed all the rice and chutney onto the leaf and offered it to Akbar. He also fetched some water from a nearby well. Akbar was quite content with the food and water and was pleased that the shepherd had shared his food with him.

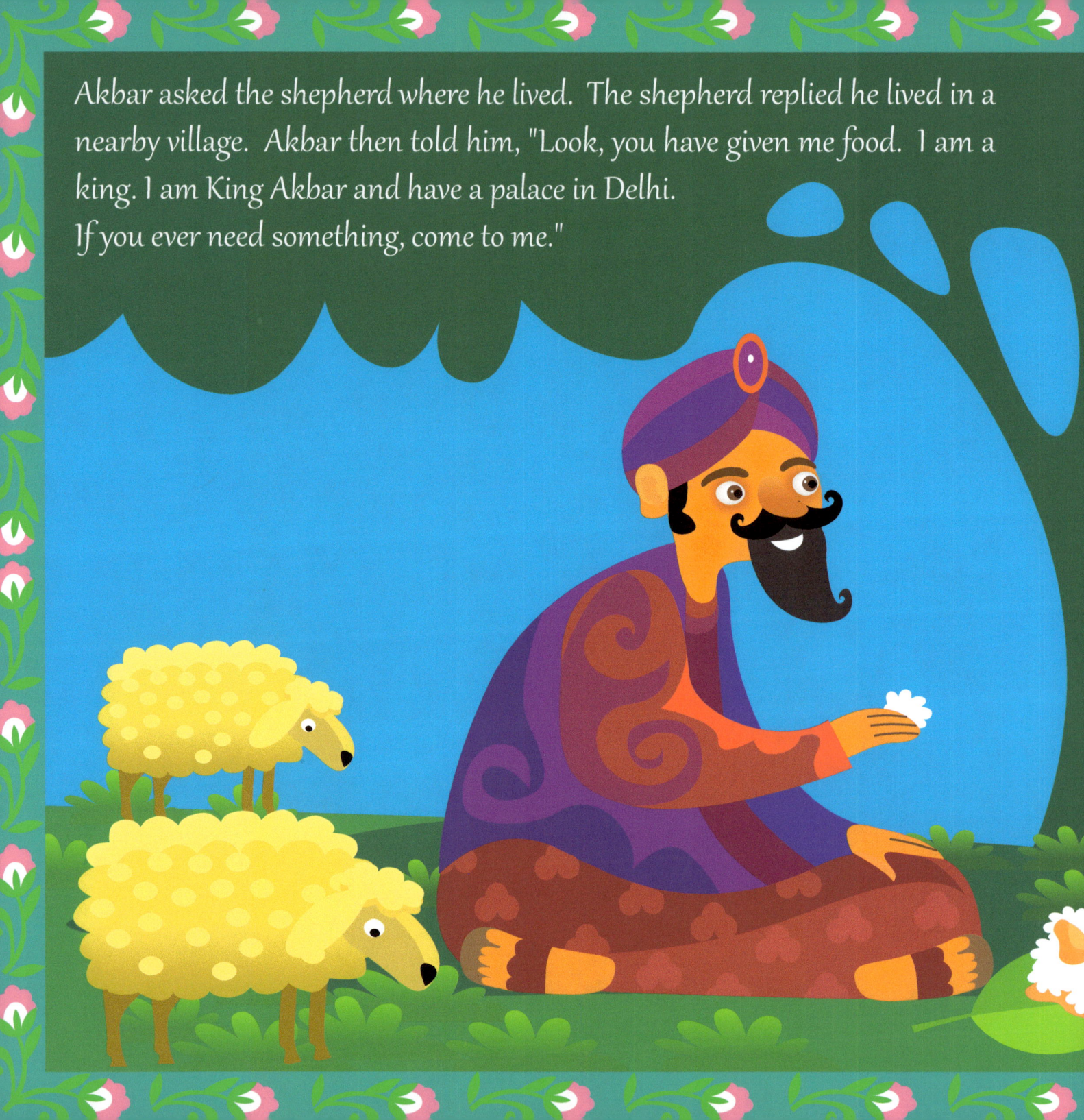

Akbar asked the shepherd where he lived. The shepherd replied he lived in a nearby village. Akbar then told him, "Look, you have given me food. I am a king. I am King Akbar and have a palace in Delhi. If you ever need something, come to me."

The shepherd was a humble person and replied, "Look, I manage with what I have. I also pay your taxes. I don't require anything from you, but if you need something from me, you can tell me."

Hearing this Akbar was delighted. He wrote down the palace address and said, "If you ever need to come to me, show this to the guards and they will not stop you and you will be able to come into my palace."

When the shepherd returned home, he told his wife he had met King Akbar and had offered him food. In return, Akbar had given him his address. He explained everything to his wife, who was a wise lady. She was delighted to know that he had met Akbar and she told her husband, "Since Akbar has asked you to meet him, you should go and request something so that our poverty will be reduced and we will be much better off."

But he was a humble shepherd and a simple man. So he told her, "How can you say this? He didn't have food and he didn't have water. He took my food and water."

But his wife insisted, "No, you go. He's a king."

For a few days the wife kept telling her husband to go meet the king. And the shepherd kept replying that whatever they had was enough.

But one fine day he agreed to meet Akbar. He carried a stick and a shawl to cover himself. On the way, it started to rain. He felt Akbar might be getting wet and bought a stack of hay to make a shelter for Akbar.

He went to the address that Akbar had given him and told the sentry, "I am a friend of Akbar and I've come to meet him."

The sentries looked at him and thought, "How could this person be a friend of Akbar?" So while they were wondering, he showed them the address given by Akbar.

The sentry checked with Akbar, who remembered this shepherd had given him food and water. The sentry then escorted the shepherd into the court of King Akbar. As he entered, he saw big mansions and the king's palace, where all of the ministers and others were seated around him.

Akbar was sitting on his throne on an elevated platform. When the shepherd entered, he saw beautiful buildings around the courtyard of King Akbar. There were golden thrones and golden seats for everyone.

He looked at Akbar and said, "O Akbar, I thought you might be sitting under a tree and I carried this bundle of hay for making a shelter for you. But you live in a palace!"

Seeing this, Akbar was very pleased. He got down from his throne and embraced the shepherd. He felt grateful that this person had given him food and now, today, he had come to build a shelter for him.

Akbar then brought him up on the throne and shared the throne with him.

After the court session was over, King Akbar took him to his home and gave him food. When the meal was over, it was time for the Muslim prayer, for namaaz.

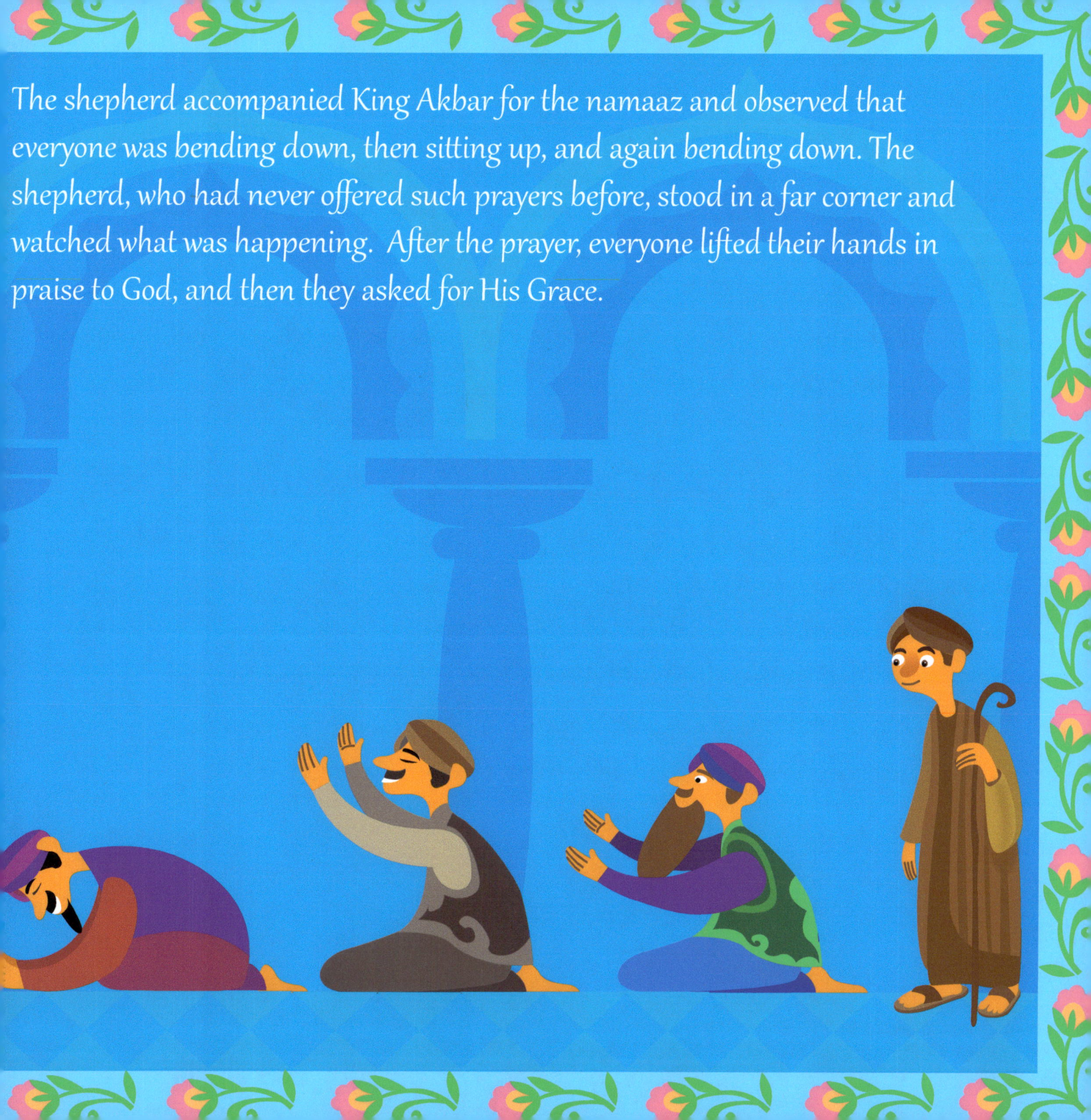

The shepherd accompanied King Akbar for the namaaz and observed that everyone was bending down, then sitting up, and again bending down. The shepherd, who had never offered such prayers before, stood in a far corner and watched what was happening. After the prayer, everyone lifted their hands in praise to God, and then they asked for His Grace.

Akbar prayed that his kingdom stay harmonious and his people remain happy, that crops grow in all the fields throughout his kingdom, and taxes continue being collected.

When the prayers were completed, they returned to Akbar's home and Akbar asked the shepherd, "Okay, you came here to meet me. Do tell me what brings you here? Do you have any need?"

Instead of answering the king's question, the shepherd asked Akbar, "O Akbar, when we went for that prayer meeting, you lifted both your hands and you were praying. So what were you doing?"

He said, "I lifted my hands to God Almighty and I was praying that my kingdom remains in good condition, that the rains are enough to produce good crops and people become more prosperous. I was praying for my kingdom and for happiness for everyone."

So the shepherd then said, "Look, you are asking me what I need. But then you are praying and you are also asking God Almighty for the things you need. So why don't you just tell me how to pray? And then I will pray to God Almighty myself. Please teach me exactly how you speak and how you pray to Him and I will also start asking in the same way."

Muslims have a long prayer, which they recite as 'La Illah Allah Hu'. So Akbar explained how that is recited. The shepherd didn't remember all of it. He just remembered the first two words, 'La Illah'. So he then said, "Okay, that is enough. I've got what I need." And then he picked up his shawl and left Akbar's palace.

While returning home from the palace, the shepherd continued repeating 'La Illah.' When he reached home, his wife looked down the road, feeling that perhaps the treasures from the king were following her husband.
But there was nothing.

So she asked him, "What happened when you met the king?"

He said, "Look, as I told you earlier. The king is a poor man. He had to come to me for eating and drinking. And when I went to his palace, I saw him praying and asking for more things from the Almighty. So as I told you before, he's not going to give us anything. We need to do it ourselves."

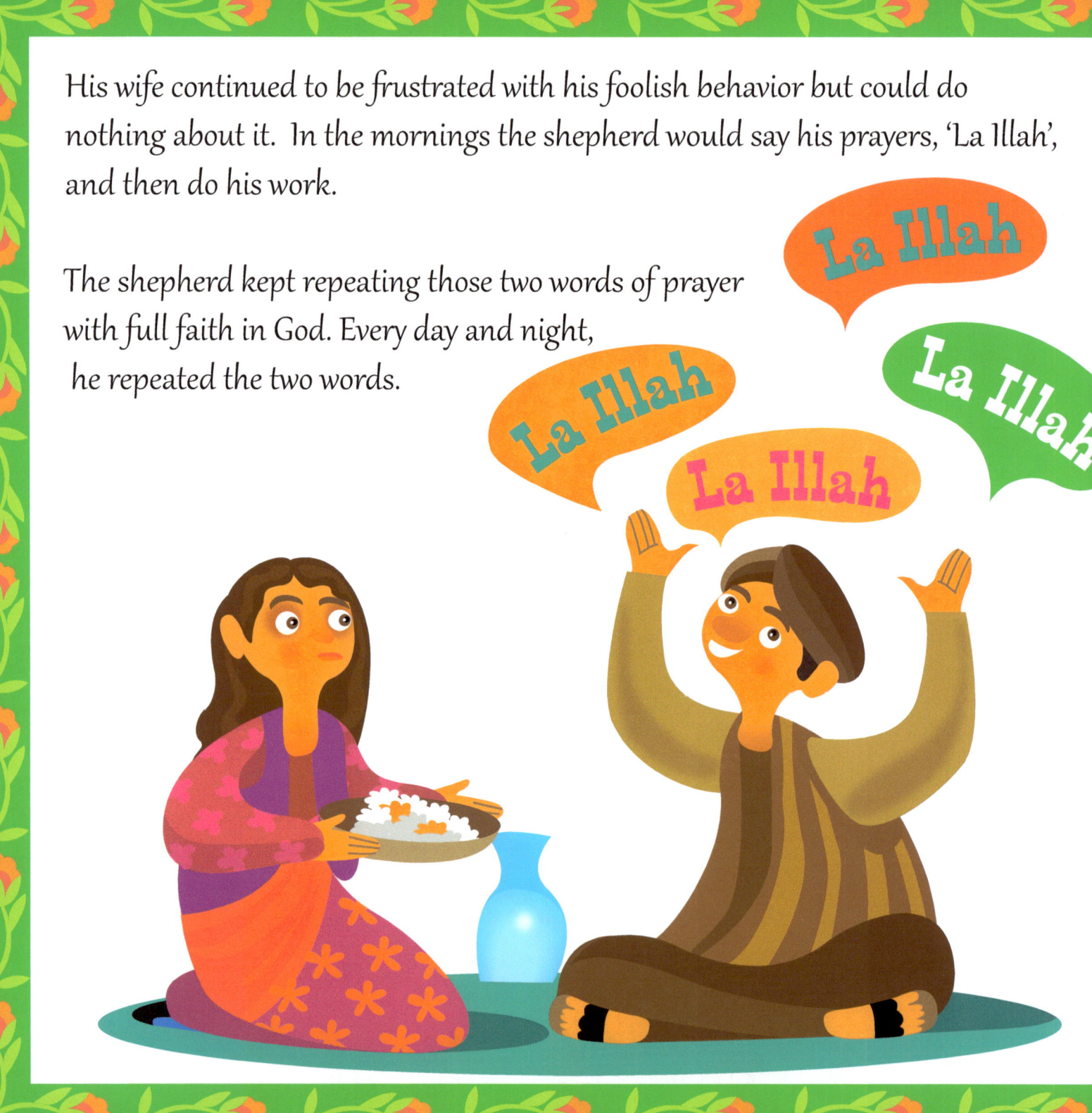

His wife continued to be frustrated with his foolish behavior but could do nothing about it. In the mornings the shepherd would say his prayers, 'La Illah', and then do his work.

The shepherd kept repeating those two words of prayer with full faith in God. Every day and night, he repeated the two words.

About four months passed with the shepherd praying every day while doing his work, and then the monsoons came.

La Illah La Illah La Illah

One evening, he went for a walk by the river near his house. He stopped to admire the view and express gratefulness to God for his life. The bank of the river had been washed away by the heavy rain, exposing three big pots, which had been buried nearby.

Close to where the shepherd stood, three thieves were sitting in a tree, waiting for nightfall to steal those pots. The shepherd was so absorbed in his prayer, he didn't see the pots or the thieves.

While he was praying, he heard a voice from one of the pots, which said, "I have to come with you, you should take me to your home!"

The shepherd replied, "If you can talk to me like this, you might as well walk to my house by yourself." And he turned to walk home.

The hidden thieves watched what was happening and wondered, "This person stood next to the pots, yet didn't take the pots with him. Something must be wrong."

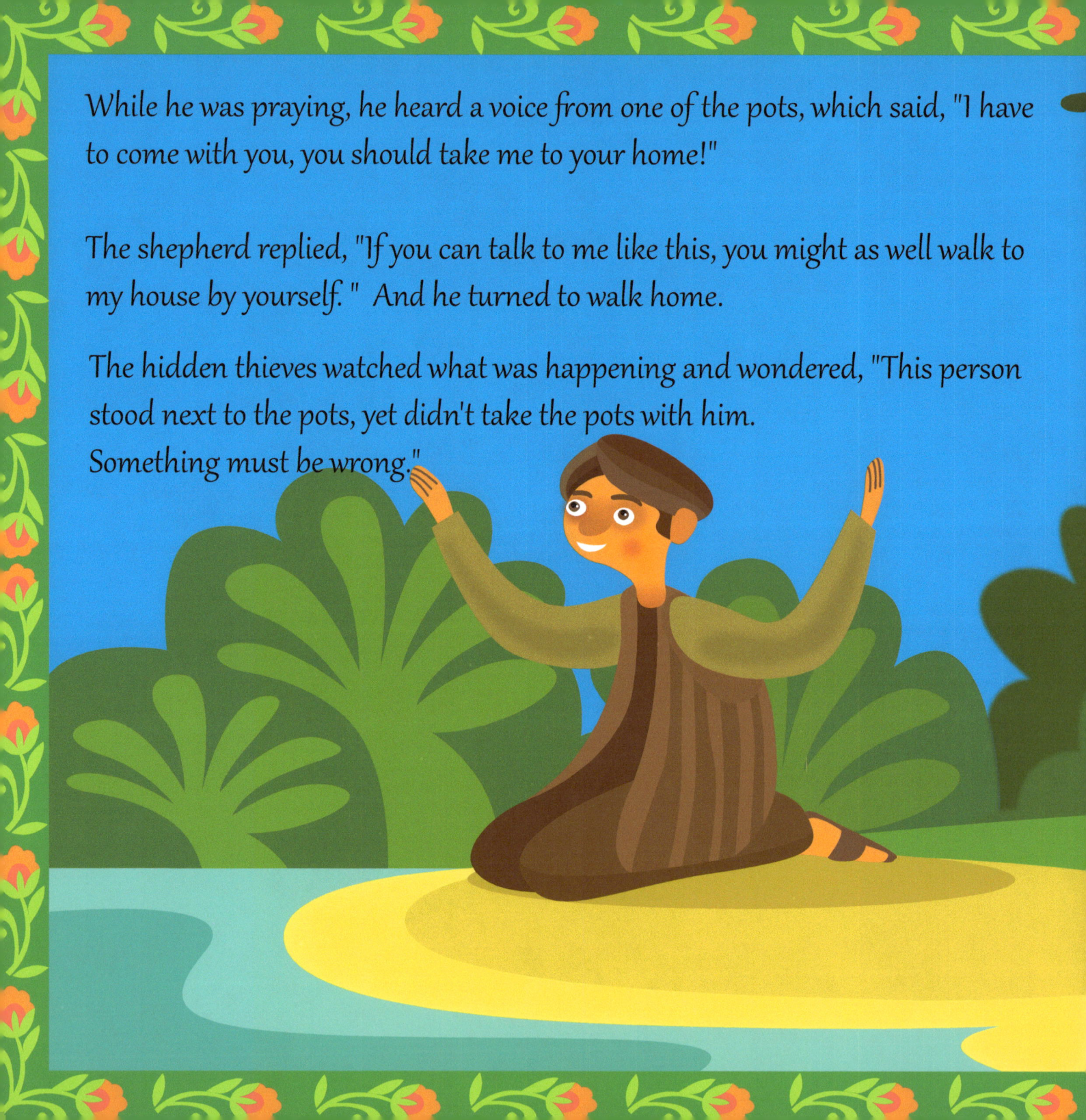

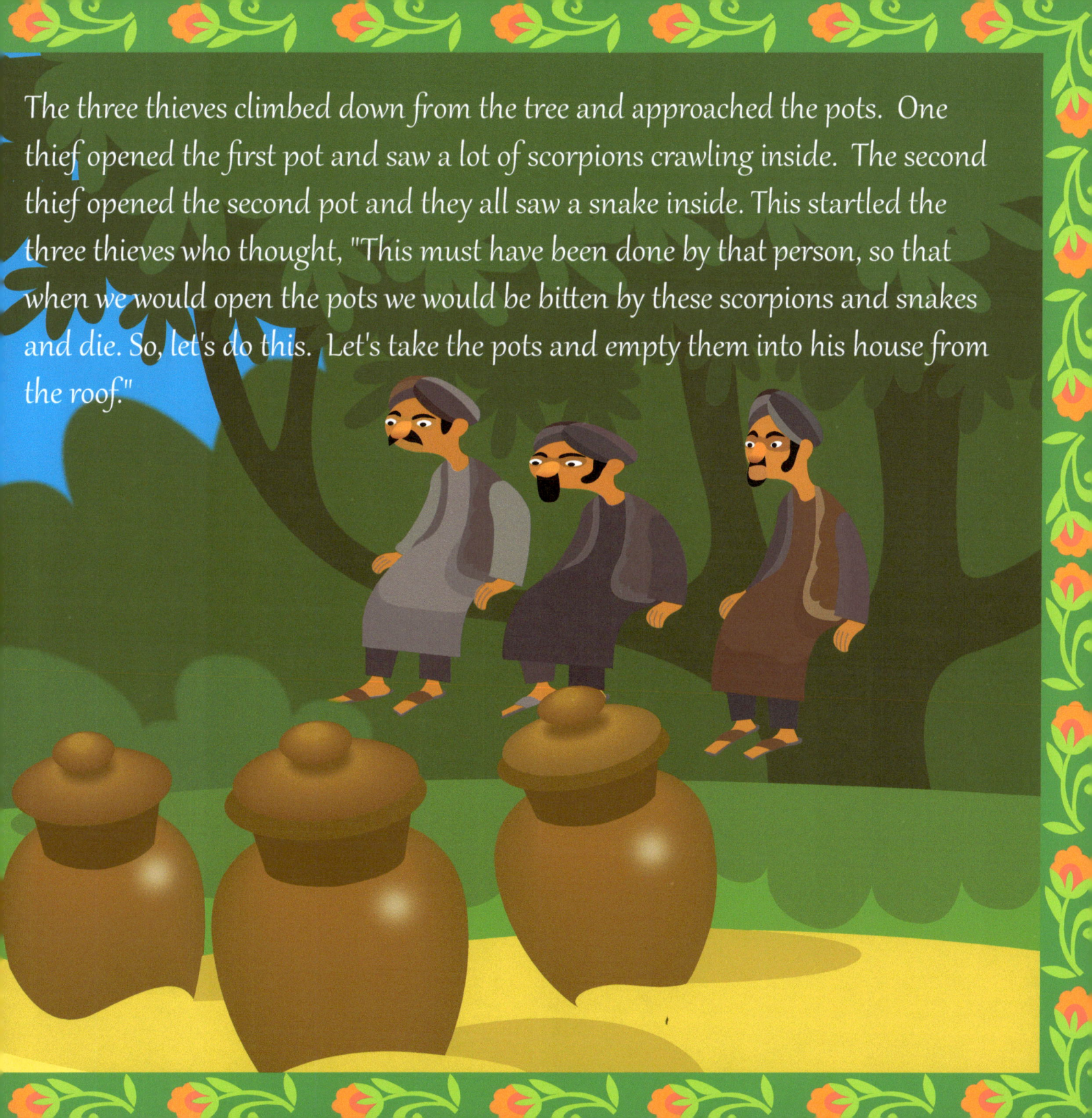

The three thieves climbed down from the tree and approached the pots. One thief opened the first pot and saw a lot of scorpions crawling inside. The second thief opened the second pot and they all saw a snake inside. This startled the three thieves who thought, "This must have been done by that person, so that when we would open the pots we would be bitten by these scorpions and snakes and die. So, let's do this. Let's take the pots and empty them into his house from the roof."

At nighttime, they went to the shepherd's house, climbed his roof, removed the tiles of the roof and then, at the same time, the thieves unloaded the contents of all three pots, which they thought were scorpions and snakes.

Everything fell inside. But it turned out that what dropped were all gems, jewelry, coins and other precious items.

The noise from the raining diamonds, rubies and assorted jewels awakened the shepherd, who woke his wife and said, "See, I told you that Allah would shower His Grace. Take whatever you want now."

With this, he became a wealthy man.
And his wife witnessed what is possible when one prays to God without worldly wants or desires.
Her husband had prayed to God with only love, affection and faith, and God listened to him and showered him with Grace.

www.ingramcontent.com/pod-product-compliance
Lightning Source LLC
Chambersburg PA
CBHW041228040426
42444CB00002B/88